Taking Care of Business
Prepared for My Loved Ones

Joe Kidd

INTRODUCTION

Imagine waking up in the middle of the night only to find your house on fire. Besides the kids and wife, what would you grab? Hundreds of thoughts cross your mind as you watch your house burn.

- Do I have copies of all my important information?
- What people do I need to call to get back on my feet?
- Can I remember all my important information?
- Do others have copies of all my important information?

Or, what if you were to have a stroke or suddenly become dependent on others. What if the worst happens, you die suddenly who would take care of your financial and personal affairs?

Would they be able to come in and get bills paid, do work on your behalf or take over yourself households finances without having to spend hours of despair, stress and uncertainty trying to figure it all out?

For these and many other reasons, it pays to have your personal financial and important information organized and at your fingertips.

This book in a proven format that many people are finding beneficial. It takes only one disaster to make you realize how important it is to gather all your family financial records in one place. Unfortunately, too many people put off this important task until it's too late

Would someone else know where your checking and savings accounts are held, what credit cards you hold, who your financial adviser is, where your safe-deposit box is, where your investments are held, who your beneficiaries are or whether you have policies that entitle your dependents to death benefits? Taking Care of Business as a road map for you and your loved ones. Combined with a folder containing important will a allow your loved ones to begin the process of taking over for you such as:

- *Estate planning and legal documents:* Wills, trusts, advance directives, powers of attorney, letters of instruction, funeral instructions
- *Financial documents:* Bank and investment statement, home mortgage, loan documents, copies of tax returns
- *Insurance document:* Copies of all insurance policies for auto, homeowners/renters, health, life, disability and long-term care
- *Personal records:* birth, adoption, citizenship, marriage, divorce and death certificates
- *Property records:* Vehicles, real estate and investments
- *Retirement planning documents:* Pension benefit statements, Social Security benefits statement and tax-deferred and individual retirement annual statements.

CONTENTS

1 PERSONAL INFORMATION

Yours

Name	
Maiden name (if Applicable)	
Social Security Number	
Date of Birth	
Place of Birth	
Mother's Name	
Mother Maiden Name	
Mother's Date of Birth	
Mother's Date of Death	
Mother's Social Security Number	
Father's Name	
Father's Date of Birth	
Father's Date of Death	
Father's Social Security Number	

Sibling's Name	Date of Birth	Phone Number	Cell Number	Address

Spouse / Domestic Partner

Name	
Maiden name (if Applicable)	
Social Security Number	
Date of Birth	
Place of Birth	
Mother's Name	
Mother Maiden Name	
Mother's Date of Birth	
Mother's Date of Death	
Mother's Social Security Number	
Father's Name	
Father's Date of Birth	
Father's Date of Death	
Father's Social Security Number	

Sibling's Name	Date of Birth	Phone Number	Cell Number	Address

2 CONTACTS

Family

Name Relationship	Date of Birth Gender	Address City State Zip	Home Phone Cell Phone	Work Phone Email Address

Friends, Neighbors, Co-workers

Name	Date of Birth	Address	Home Phone	Work Phone
Relationship	Gender	City State Zip	Cell Phone	Email Address

Professional

Type of Professional Name / Company Name	Address City State Zip	Phone Email Address
Attorney		
Will executor		
Stockbroker		
Money Manager		
Finance Advisor		
Accountant		
Insurance Agent		
Doctor (PCP)		
Doctor (Specialist)		

Professional (continued)

Type of Professional Name / Company Name	Address City State Zip	Phone Email Address

Employee Benefits

Company Name:					Benefits Contact Number:		
Open Enrollment Period:					Date Last Updated:		

Health Insurance

GroupID	Employee ID	Deductible	Co-insurance	Max Out of Pocket	Premium	HSA Contribution

Special Conditions:

Exclusions:

Dental

Premium		Coverage Details	

Vision

Premium		Coverage Details	

Health Care Flexible Spending Account (FSA)

Contribution		Coverage Details	

Health Care Saving Account (HSA)

Contribution		Coverage Details	

Family Care Plan

Contribution		Coverage Details	

Basic Life Insurance and Accidental Death and Dismemberment (AD&D)

Premium		Coverage Details	

Supplement Employee Life Insurance and AD&D

Premium		Coverage Details	

Spouse / domestic Partner Life and AD&D			
Premium		Coverage Details	

Employee Critical Illness			
Premium		Coverage Details	

Spouse / domestic partner Critical Illness			
Premium		Coverage Details	

Accident Protection Plan			
Premium		Coverage Details	

Pet Insurance			
Premium		Coverage Details	

Legal Insurance			
		Coverage Details	

3 Financial And Bank Accounts

Type	Company Name	Address	Account # / PIN	Names On Account

Safe Deposit Boxes

Bank Name	Address	Box Number	Names of Box	Key Location

4 LOANS

Lender Name:					
Address:		Phone:			
Account Number		Collateral			
Loan Amount:		Loan Term:		Monthly payment:	
Payoff Date:		Credit life		Credit Disability	
Document Location::					

Lender Name:					
Address:		Phone:			
Account Number		Collateral			
Loan Amount:		Loan Term:		Monthly payment:	
Payoff Date:		Credit life		Credit Disability	
Document Location:					

Lender Name:					
Address:		Phone:			
Account Number		Collateral			
Loan Amount:		Loan Term:		Monthly payment:	
Payoff Date:		Credit life		Credit Disability	
Document Location:					

Lender Name:					
Address:		Phone:			
Account Number		Collateral			
Loan Amount:		Loan Term:		Monthly payment:	
Payoff Date:		Credit life		Credit Disability	
Document Location:					

Lender Name:					
Address:		Phone:			
Account Number		Collateral			
Loan Amount:		Loan Term:		Monthly payment:	
Payoff Date:		Credit life		Credit Disability	
Document Location:					

Lender Name:					
Address:		Phone:			
Account Number		Collateral			
Loan Amount:		Loan Term:		Monthly payment:	
Payoff Date:		Credit life		Credit Disability	
Document Location:					

Lender Name::					
Address:		Phone:			
Account Number		Collateral			
Loan Amount:		Loan Term:		Monthly payment:	
Payoff Date:		Credit life		Credit Disability	
Document Location::					

Lender Name:					
Address:		Phone:			
Account Number		Collateral			
Loan Amount:		Loan Term:		Monthly payment:	
Payoff Date:		Credit life		Credit Disability	
Document Location::					

Lender Name:					
Address:		Phone:			
Account Number		Collateral			
Loan Amount:		Loan Term:		Monthly payment:	
Payoff Date:		Credit life		Credit Disability	
Document Location::					

Lender Name:					
Address:		Phone:			
Account Number		Collateral			
Loan Amount:		Loan Term:		Monthly payment:	
Payoff Date:		Credit life		Credit Disability	
Document Location:					

Lender Name:			
Address:		Phone:	
Account Number		Collateral	
Loan Amount:	Loan Term:	Monthly payment:	
Payoff Date:	Credit life	Credit Disability	
Document Location:			

Lender Name:			
Address:		Phone:	
Account Number		Collateral	
Loan Amount:	Loan Term:	Monthly payment:	
Payoff Date:	Credit life	Credit Disability	
Document Location:			

Lender Name:			
Address:		Phone:	
Account Number		Collateral	
Loan Amount:	Loan Term:	Monthly payment:	
Payoff Date:	Credit life	Credit Disability	
Document Location:			

Lender Name:			
Address:		Phone:	
Account Number		Collateral	
Loan Amount:	Loan Term:	Monthly payment:	
Payoff Date:	Credit life	Credit Disability	
Document Location:			

Lender Name:			
Address:		Phone:	
Account Number		Collateral	
Loan Amount:	Loan Term:	Monthly payment:	
Payoff Date:	Credit life	Credit Disability	
Document Location:			

5 CREDIT CARDS

In Your Name

Issued By	Card Type	Account Number	PIN	Interest Rate	Credit Limit	Contact Number

In Your Spouse / Domestic Partners Name

Issued By	Card Type	Account Number	PIN	Interest Rate	Credit Limit	Contact Number

6 PERSONAL INSURNACE

Type of Insurance:		Policy number:	
Company Name:		Agent Name:	
Address:		Phone Number:	
Website:		Claims Phone Number:	
Coverage Summary			

Type of Insurance:		Policy number:	
Company Name:		Agent Name:	
Address:		Phone Number:	
Website:		Claims Phone Number:	
Coverage Summary			

Type of Insurance:		Policy number:	
Company Name:		Agent Name:	
Address:		Phone Number:	
Website:		Claims Phone Number:	
Coverage Summary			

Type of Insurance:		Policy number:	
Company Name:		Agent Name:	
Address:		Phone Number:	
Website:		Claims Phone Number:	
Coverage Summary			

Type of Insurance:		Policy number:	
Company Name:		Agent Name:	
Address:		Phone Number:	
Website:		Claims Phone Number:	
Coverage Summary			

Type of Insurance:		Policy number:	
Company Name:		Agent Name:	
Address:		Phone Number:	
Website:		Claims Phone Number:	
Coverage Summary			

Type of Insurance:		Policy number:	
Company Name:		Agent Name:	
Address:		Phone Number:	
Website:		Claims Phone Number:	
Coverage Summary			

Type of Insurance:		Policy number:	
Company Name:		Agent Name:	
Address:		Phone Number:	
Website:		Claims Phone Number:	
Coverage Summary			

Type of Insurance:		Policy number:	
Company Name:		Agent Name:	
Address:		Phone Number:	
Website:		Claims Phone Number:	
Coverage Summary			

Type of Insurance:		Policy number:	
Company Name:		Agent Name:	
Address:		Phone Number:	
Website:		Claims Phone Number:	
Coverage Summary			

Type of Insurance:		Policy number:	
Company Name:		Agent Name:	
Address:		Phone Number:	
Website:		Claims Phone Number:	
Coverage Summary			

Type of Insurance:		Policy number:	
Company Name:		Agent Name:	
Address:		Phone Number:	
Website:		Claims Phone Number:	
Coverage Summary			

Type of Insurance:		Policy number:	
Company Name:		Agent Name:	
Address:		Phone Number:	
Website:		Claims Phone Number:	
Coverage Summary			

Type of Insurance:		Policy number:	
Company Name:		Agent Name:	
Address:		Phone Number:	
Website:		Claims Phone Number:	
Coverage Summary			

Type of Insurance:		Policy number:	
Company Name:		Agent Name:	
Address:		Phone Number:	
Website:		Claims Phone Number:	
Coverage Summary			

Type of Insurance:		Policy number:	
Company Name:		Agent Name:	
Address:		Phone Number:	
Website:		Claims Phone Number:	
Coverage Summary			

Type of Insurance:		Policy number:	
Company Name:		Agent Name:	
Address:		Phone Number:	
Website:		Claims Phone Number:	
Coverage Summary			

Type of Insurance:		Policy number:	
Company Name:		Agent Name:	
Address:		Phone Number:	
Website:		Claims Phone Number:	
Coverage Summary			

Type of Insurance:		Policy number:	
Company Name:		Agent Name:	
Address:		Phone Number:	
Website:		Claims Phone Number:	
Coverage Summary			

Type of Insurance:		Policy number:	
Company Name:		Agent Name:	
Address:		Phone Number:	
Website:		Claims Phone Number:	
Coverage Summary			

7 INVESTMENTS

Stocks, Bonds and Securities

Asset Name	Serial Number	Date Purchased	Purchase Price	Qty	Other Information

Mutual Funds

Company Name	Id Number	Date Purchased	Purchase Price	Qty	Other Information

8 RETIREMENT ACCOUNTS

Account Type	Date Invested	Company Name	Address	Phone	Amount

9 ONLINE ACCOUNTS AND PASSWORDS

Account	Website	Username	Password	Security Question Answers

Account	Website	Username	Password	Security Question Answers

JOE KIDD

Account	Website	Username	Password	Security Question Answers

Account	Website	Username	Password	Security Question Answers

JOE KIDD

Account	Website	Username	Password	Security Question Answers